SIR WILLIAM LYONS ON JAGUAR

Published in June 2025

ISBN 978-1-910505-99-1

Published by Evro Publishing, Westrow House, Holwell, Sherborne, Dorset DT9 5LF, UK

Design by Julian Balme at Vegas Design

Printed and bound in India by Imprint Press

www.evropublishing.com

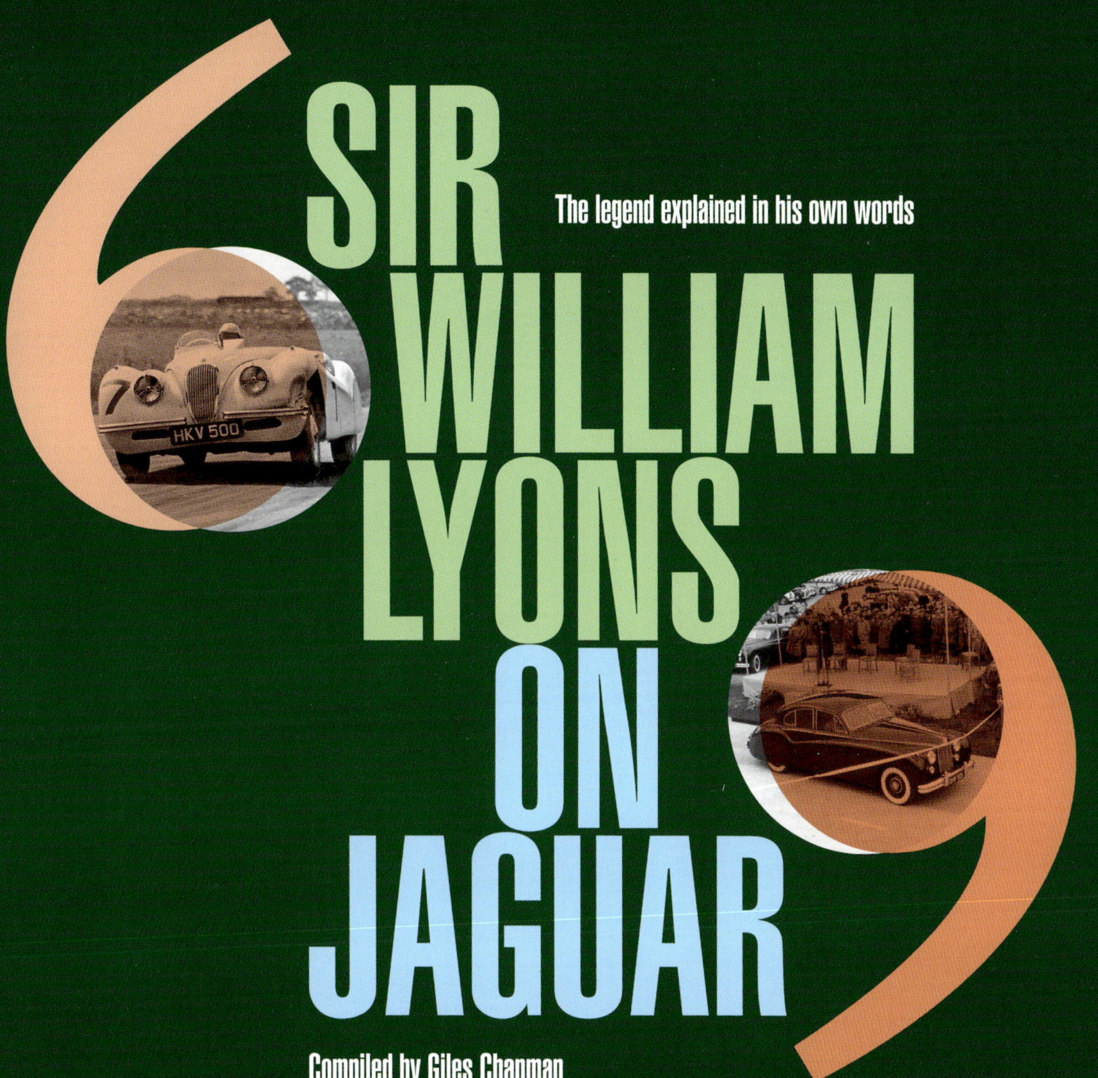

SIR WILLIAM LYONS ON JAGUAR

The legend explained in his own words

Compiled by Giles Chapman

Like many enthusiasts, I love Jaguar cars, and I have the utmost admiration for Sir William Lyons, the founder and driving force behind this world-famous British marque.

INTRODUCTION

By Giles Chapman

This year, 2025, marks the 40th anniversary of his passing, and it is safe to say that – so far – his like has not been seen again. How did he do it all? Sadly, it is now much too late to settle down for an in-depth conversation to find out.

Sir William, anyway, rarely opened up. He gave few interviews and had an old-fashioned formality which meant he kept his opinions to himself. So when I chanced upon the text of a 1969 speech where he told his own story in greater detail than I'd ever read anywhere else, I was spellbound. At a time when Jaguar itself is at a pivotal stage in its history, it is fascinating and enlightening to have Sir William's very own reflections on its genesis.

The simple rationale of this book is to share his spoken words with the wider Jaguar-supporting community for the first time, by reproducing them exactly as they were delivered on that long-forgotten afternoon. I hope they stand as a valuable addition to Jaguar's recorded history that can now be accessed by everyone; in a book that's different to the numerous others already published on both Jaguar and Lyons himself.

By way of an explanation and for context, I have added a detailed Commentary following the faithful transcript, which also examines the post-Lyons era of Jaguar right up to its dramatic, controversial and imminent rebirth.

I am indebted to the late ex-British Leyland PR executive Clive Richardson, whose presence of mind meant an original copy of the speech was stored in his files, which it was my responsibility to dispose of after his sad passing. I know he would have been happy to see this book.

I'm also extremely fortunate to enjoy the friendship of Michael Quinn, via the Royal Automobile Club, who graciously wrote the Foreword for us. Michael is Sir William's grandson and patron of the Jaguar Daimler Heritage Trust, and he writes movingly of time spent with his grandfather, and his own admiration for the man's immense achievements. My respectful thanks extend to the wider Lyons and Quinn families too.

The rest of this book's creation is a wonderful confluence of publishing talents who have teamed up to make it real. I am very grateful to Julian Balme for his beautiful design, and to Eric Verdon-Roe and Mark Hughes at Evro Publishing for agreeing that this book is a unique project worth getting behind.

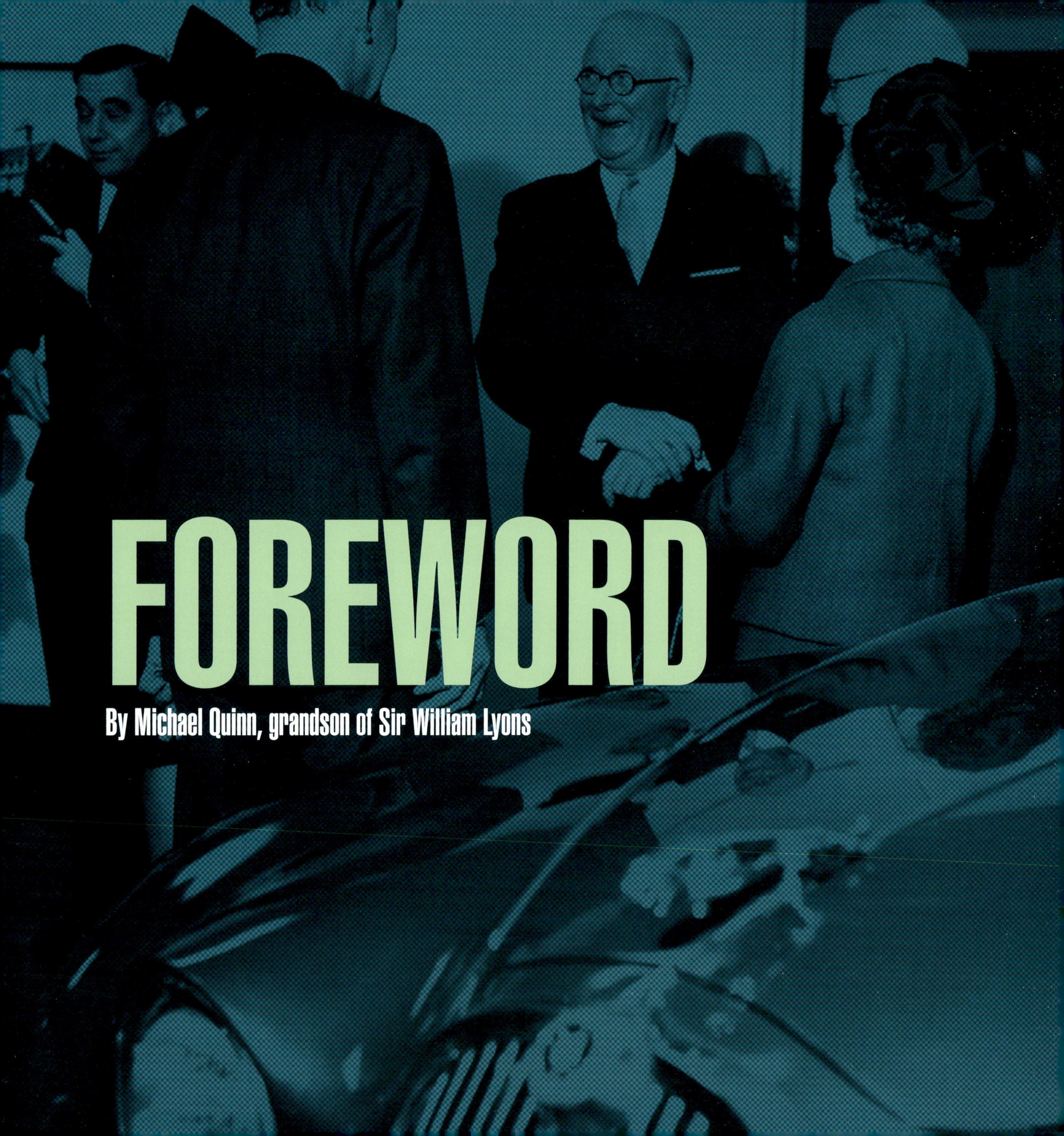

FOREWORD

By Michael Quinn, grandson of Sir William Lyons

This address, delivered to the Institute of the Motor Industry by my grandfather at Church House, Westminster in London one afternoon in April 1969, is a fascinating insight into the history of Jaguar. This is because it is his own story – as he saw it, told by him. Despite having a very competent PR department at Jaguar, there is detail in this paper that tells me these are my grandfather's personal reflections, and could not have been written by anyone else. I think it has real interest and all the more power for that.

Listening to a recording of the occasion, it strikes me as being a very formal affair, in very formal surroundings. It is quite long and very wordy, and must have been a little intimidating to deliver even to someone of my grandfather's experience in the industry. He was not comfortable speaking in public, and occasionally he does seem to struggle a bit with his voice to deliver it.

Points of interest for me are that he appears to concede that producing the XK engine was a gamble, and the perceived wisdom of the time did not expect it to succeed. Thank goodness he took that risk, as it did pay off handsomely indeed. Another point of note – and in a room of motor industrialists I detect some pride here – is how by 1964 Jaguar had paid out over £2m to its shareholders, and achieved a valuation of £16m; all with an investment of just £185,000 into the business since its inception.

When I look back upon the achievements of my grandfather, I still find myself somewhat lost in admiration for what he created. From humble beginnings producing sidecars, in four decades he had formed a company with global appeal and respect, that had won Le Mans on five occasions, and was simultaneously the choice of monarchs. I cannot imagine how much focus and dedication it must have taken to achieve that, especially when one recalls that he retained total control over all aspects of the business and its output.

Even as majority shareholder and Chairman of the Board, all inter-departmental correspondence crossed his desk, usually in the form of memos, as he sought to negotiate the increasingly complex issues that faced him. He took a personal interest in responding to all communication, from letters by senior executives abroad seeking improved renumeration, to letters from outraged citizens

of London complaining about the high speeds achievable by the E-type, young boys expressing admiration of the latest Mark X saloon, episodes involving a lack of engine sump washers on the production line, to the quality of the company Christmas cards being dispatched. Most numerous of all correspondence were the relentless calls from importers and dealers for more cars to satisfy demand, and in this aim he was regularly thwarted by battles with the unions to keep the production lines open despite strike action.

And then – and this is where his greatest satisfaction lay – the creation of beautiful cars. He had no experience, training or background in car design; he was no artist, and yet artistically he created some of the world's most revered cars. He didn't work alone in this, relying on craftsmen to help him create full-size prototypes, and he did not design the racing cars, but he retained control over all the projects and every detail was subject to his personal approval and sign-off. This was vital to him to retain control of the output and ensure it met with his own refined personal taste – there was too much at stake to risk otherwise.

My own recollections of him are of a modest and quiet man, very happy in very comfortable surroundings, but that he shunned any form of ostentation or showiness. He was quite formal in appearance and demeanour, and as a young lad I was somewhat overawed by him, if I am honest. Quite apart from his accomplishments, which dawned upon me gradually as I grew older, he was a figure who commanded no small measure of respect. There was a formality about him, stemming I suspect from his own Edwardian upbringing, but at the same time a warmheartedness which always shone through. And he was devoted to his wife Greta.

As children, my sister and I spent many happy times at their home, Wappenbury Hall, playing in the many rooms and in the extensive grounds. Always, however, was the need to heed the warnings about keeping away from the expertly manicured flowerbeds. Riding bicycles was a joy to be confined to the many paths, and definitely not riding over the perfect edges of the lawns. All meals were conducted properly at the dinner table with one's manners always closely observed (and commented on if found wanting), and yet I

OPPOSITE TOP Jaguar D-type crosses the line to win the 1956 24 Hours of Le Mans.

OPPOSITE BELOW The Jaguar 420G.

BELOW Jaguar XK150 roadster, known as the 'Open' version.

also remember him sitting me on his knee and helping me to learn to read. I was very proud one year when he turned up at my school to watch me run in the annual sports day, although characteristically he mingled with the other parents anonymously. I recall now that running at school was one of the activities in which he shone, and I know now where I may have got my own turn of speed from.

My grandfather's stated aim was to establish a successful business venture creating motor cars that were 'pleasing to the eye'. The fact that he was so spectacularly successful in that aim stems, I suspect, from the fact that he was so enthusiastic in that task, and, more importantly, he enthused those he picked as his team to share that passion. That this 'business venture' came to mean so much more than that, to so many people, is a testament to that teamwork and the inspiration and flair for the motor car which my grandfather possessed.

Michael Quinn
London, May 2025

THE HISTORY OF JAGUAR AND...

EYX 262

THE FUTURE OF THE SPECIALISED CAR...

IN THE BRITISH MOTOR INDUSTRY

By Sir William Lyons

JAGUAR

OPPOSITE Jaguar Mk X, the epitome of 1960s British style.

LEFT William Lyons on a Harley-Davidson, early 1920s.

HISTORY

What I have to say in my paper today is of a rather different character to the papers read to you by my predecessors. This is because I have been expressly invited by your President to speak to you about the history of Jaguar and the role of the specialist car, both of which subjects have, of course, a special interest for me. I am, therefore, conscious that I may express myself in greater detail than perhaps I should in a paper of this kind, and I hope that you will forgive me if what I have to say introduces a large element of my personal experiences. It would take longer than the time available to me this afternoon to give you a complete history, so I have confined myself to what I have felt are the highlights in the growth of the company.

I think it is appropriate that, in presenting to you a picture of the history of Jaguar, I should start in the year 1922, when I joined with a partner in Blackpool to make Swallow sidecars for motor cycles. We started with three men and a boy – the latter, incidentally, is still with Jaguar in a senior position. We started with an overdraft of £1000 provided by guarantees of £500 each by our respective fathers. I am afraid it proved very inadequate but, by repeated appeals for help to the manager of the bank, which I visited each Saturday morning for the wages (I usually arrived after the bank had closed and often kept the workpeople waiting), I managed to keep paying the mounting accounts, and the business on an even keel. I will always appreciate the confidence of the bank manager in allowing the overdraft to exceed the guarantee by a considerable margin.

It proved to be a successful business within the limits of the potential markets, and it was these limitations which, in 1927, turned my thoughts to building a body on the Austin Seven chassis, which Sir Herbert Austin had brought out. The conception of this car had a strong appeal, except that the body was a very stark affair, albeit very practical, It provided reasonable seating for four people and was wonderful value for money. I believed that it would also appeal to a lot of people if it had a more luxurious and attractive body. We therefore bought one of these chassis and produced the Austin Swallow, an open sports two-seater and, in the following year, a saloon model; both had their own special radiator cowling and looked very different from the ordinary Austin. I took the saloon up to London to show to Henlys – a new, forward-thinking and quickly growing business. They immediately gave me an order for 500 cars – we sold it as a complete car – but stipulated that they, Henlys, should have the distribution south of a line drawn from and including Bristol to the Wash. I did not know how on earth we were going to make 500 but I accepted the order with alacrity, and indeed considerable amazement. I also agreed to the territory for which they asked. My visit to Henlys was the occasion of my first meeting with Frank Hough and Bertie Henly, the two partners. Hough was a dynamic man with a determination to do things quickly; Henly was the steadying influence and he was also the finest salesman I have ever met. I recall that, during my visit to their showroom, then 91 Great Portland Street, a salesman came up to Bert Henly and said he had a customer who wished to buy a second-hand Austin, which was standing in the showroom, but he could not afford to pay the £350 which was being asked for the car. "Could Mr Henly make any reduction?" the salesman asked. After some discussion, Bertie Henly agreed to accept £325 but the salesman returned to say the customer still could not afford it, whereupon Henly said, "let me have a go at him." I was an interested spectator whilst the discussion was taking place, and when Henly returned he said to the salesman: "take him into the office and get his cheque for a new Alvis." This satisfied me that, if anyone could sell Austin Swallows, it was Henlys.

I returned to Blackpool full of exuberance and I had little sleep for the next six months as chassis arrived at Blackpool railway station in numbers with which we could not cope – the station yard was full and the station master was raising hell. There was nothing for it but to get into larger premises – we could hardly call the one we occupied a factory.

OPPOSITE Lyons acknowledges the salesmanship of Henlys in Swallow's early success.

BELOW Henlys produced rapturous marketing that made the S.S. 1 desirable.

BELOW S.S. 1 and its long bonnet boasted 'The £1000 look for £310'.

OPPOSITE Swallow's display at the London Motor Show, Olympia in 1929.

We had already found that our supply lines were too extended and the type of labour we wanted had to come from the Midlands, so I went to Coventry to see what I could find and, after several days' search, found a disused shell-filling factory. This was one of four separate buildings. Two of them were occupied by a firm of body builders, supplying fabric-covered bodies to Hillman, the other two were vacant and I was interested in one of these. The building was actually on the market for sale, but as we had no capital to buy it, I managed to persuade the owners to lease it to us at a reasonable rent. It was five times larger than the premises we occupied in Blackpool and I felt it was a tremendous step forward. It was in terrible condition and the contractor's price for repairing and repainting it was more than the total value of our own net assets, so we engaged a lot of labourers and did the job ourselves for a fraction of the cost. So, in September 1928 we moved, lock, stock and barrel from Blackpool.

RIGHT S.S. Jaguar saloons ready for shipment abroad outside the Foleshill, Coventry factory.

Arthur Whittaker, who later became general manager and then a director, and finally deputy chairman, headed the advanced contingent; he telephoned me on arrival to say that the main electric feed cable to the factory had been stolen, something I found difficult to believe, but it was unfortunately true and it cost us £1200 to have it replaced. However, we soon settled down and got production moving.

It was a most exciting time. We worked from 8 o'clock in the morning until 11 or 12 at night, for we aimed to raise production from 12 a week to 50 a week within three months. We knew we could only do this by adopting a new method of coachbuilt construction, all bodies made in this country in those days were coachbuilt. Whereas in Blackpool each body-maker had been responsible for the complete framing-up of the body, the latest method used for volume production was the machining of the wooden parts in specially constructed jigs, so that they could be assembled rather like a jigsaw puzzle. This saved a tremendous amount of labour, but the introduction of the method caused us many headaches. In fact, we were in such trouble at one time that the body-makers approached me en-bloc and told me that the whole thing was too complicated and doomed to failure, and that we should resort to the old method. We persevered knowing that the economies could be very considerable and before Christmas we had achieved our 50 bodies a week. We were really in business!

NO SMOKING
4E 51312
51312
BLACK

OPPOSITE The Browns Lane plant humming with E-type assembly, 1960s.

BELOW Cowl of the Austin Swallow only just fitted the radiator…

One of the reasons for the profitability of the Austin Swallow was a system of wage payment which ensured that the amount provided in our price build-up for labour costs was not exceeded – a state of affairs I would be very happy to see today!

Firstly we made a time-study of all the operations, very much as modern practice, although it was done more crudely. Of course, we only had to deal with body build, trim and paint, and then mount the body on the chassis as it came to us from the Austin company. However, unbeknown to them, we had to do one or two modifications to accommodate our body design. I recall that one of these was needed because the radiator filler neck was half an inch too high for our special radiator cowl. We solved this problem by placing a block of wood on the top of the filler neck and striking it a sharp blow which resulted in a very neat depression in the brass radiator header tank, thus lowering the filler neck to the required height. I am sure Sir Herbert Austin, as he was then, would not have approved, although it was a perfectly sound job – even if the methods were somewhat unconventional by engineering standards.

However, all operations were priced according to the time factor involved, to give an earning rate of about £5 per week, which was very good pay in those days and equivalent to a wage of £40 per week today. We then printed books of vouchers – one book for each car – each voucher covering one or more operation. The value of the vouchers varied in accordance with the price at which the operation had been costed. Upon completion of an operation, or when convenient, the operator, who wrote his name on the place provided on the voucher, presented it to the foreman for his signature and authorisation for payment. At the end of each day, the vouchers were handed in, and all the only wages clerk we then employed had to do was to add up the value of each man's vouchers and pay him accordingly on Friday night. On all the factory walls were large notices which said 'No daywork paid'.

Yes, we did have occasional labour problems, even in those days, but they were quickly resolved to everyone's satisfaction. For instance, when we came to Coventry the additional labour we engaged during the first week did not take very kindly to the methods I have described and they endeavoured to break us from them by storming into the stores, and distributing the contents of the parts bins on the floor, as a demonstration of their objection. We dealt with this outbreak by simply saying – "that is the system we work, if you do not like it you need not work here." Only a few left and within a couple of weeks everyone

The beauty

Was beauty in car design ever
expressed in such striking fashion
in the 1933 S.S.? Olympia wil
emphasize that its individualit
distinction are beyond comparisor
A full four-seater Saloon with slidin
comprehensive and tasteful equi
the S.S.I is a car to be desired
motorist of discrimination. Lu
interior, with quickly adjustable c

STAND 147

Manufacturers:
THE SWALLOW COACHBUILDING CO., LTD.
FOLESHILL, COVENTRY. Coventry 8027

was earning good money, particularly as we often worked well into the night. We had a wonderful enthusiasm and to achieve the output target for the day was a challenge to all.

So successful was this venture that by the summer of 1929 we had acquired the adjacent factory and had commenced to produce the Standard Swallow, Swift Swallow, Fiat Swallow and Wolseley Hornet Swallow, all of which raised our production to something like 100 per week, and we had started to make really good profits which we ploughed back into the business.

A great deal of the body designs we had used were dictated by chassis design and, therefore, I badly wanted to produce a chassis which did not inhibit body design to such a degree. So, in 1930, we designed a chassis frame which would accommodate the Standard 16 or 20h.p. engines, suspension and transmission. Rubery Owen made it for us and R.W. Maudslay, who was then chairman and managing director of the Standard Motor Company, agreed to supply the complete chassis using this special frame. This was about the time that John Black joined Standards from Hillmans as general manager. This hybrid was to be called the S.S. 1, a name which was agreed upon after a long argument with Maudslay and Black, which resulted from my determination to establish a marque of our own. There was much speculation as to whether S.S. stood for Standard Swallow or Swallow Special – it was never resolved. We introduced this car at the 1931 Olympia Motor Show and its low line and

long bonnet caused quite a sensation. Harold Pemberton of the *Daily Express* had been up to the works two days before the Show opened which resulted, to my amazement, in a huge picture occupying nearly all the front page of the *Daily Express*, with banner headlines describing the car as 'The car with the £1000 look for £310'. The Show was a great success and we signed up distributors and dealers all over the country – many of them still represent us.

The car, unfortunately, did not quite live up to the promise of its appearance for by no means could the engine be described as a good performer for its capacity. I was sure, however, that the way was now clear for a complete car of our own – not only had it to be a good-looker, but also it had to have an exceptionally good performance. So we started to design a completely new body and, at the same time, we called in Harry Weslake to design for us an overhead-valve cylinder head for the Standard Motor Company's 6 cylinder side valve engine which had a seven-bearing crankshaft and basically was very good. We used the same block, covering up the valve chest with a plate, and it made a good-looking unit. But, more than that, it had a very good performance.

ABOVE Unlike many rivals, at first Jaguar had to adapt other people's engines; yet by the 1970s it was building the world's only mass-produced V12.

OPPOSITE No directions needed; the S.S. 1 Tourer of 1934 showed Lyons was on his way.

TRING STATION
ALDBURY
IVINGHOE
NEW GROUND
PHONE
CROSS ROADS
TELEPHONE
AND
FIRE
EXTINGUISHER
DAY & NIGHT
BY USE OF
A A MEMBERS KEY
HEADQUARTERS
FANUM HOUSE
BLL 267

MWK 959

OPPOSITE Lyons would never be outsmarted by the bombastic Sir John Black, seen here with a Standard Eight.

BELOW Some of Lyons' key trusted people, left to right: Malcolm Sayer, William Heynes, Bob Knight, Ron Sutton, Arthur Ramsey, Keith Cambage and, seated, Norman Dewis.

Now, we had the cylinder head design, but we had no machine shop in which to make it. So I talked to John Black, who was more-or-less running the Standard Motor Company, Maudslay having been quick to realise his capabilities, and Black agreed to put in the plant to make the new head and supply the engine complete. This proved to be an ideal arrangement.

All this coincided with the arrival of W.M. Heynes, who joined us from Humber, and who was to become chief engineer, and later vice chairman (engineering). He was entrusted with the design of chassis and all three new units – body, engine and chassis – came together as the first S.S. Jaguar. It was a really good car. When we introduced it to our distributors and dealers at the Mayfair Hotel, we displayed it on a stage and asked the seated audience to write their estimate of the selling price of the car, on a card which was handed to each of them. With two scrutinisers from the gathering as supervisors, a comptometer operator calculated the average of all the prices handed in. This came to £765, so when I announced that the actual price was £395 it created quite a lot of excitement and, indeed, added much enthusiasm for the car.

RIGHT The S.S. 100 proved perfect for competition, such as here on the 1937 Monte Carlo Rally.

OVERLEAF Unveiling in 1961 of the E-type for the US market, where slightly confusingly it would be known as the XKE.

A derivative of this was the S.S. Jaguar 100, which was based on a shortened version of the new chassis, with a very practical two-seater sports body. We did produce an interim model with the side valve engine called the S.S. 90 but it was soon replaced by the S.S. 100. The new engine in this car produced 40 h.p. per litre which, outside the racing car field, was outstandingly good in those days and gave the S.S. 100 a performance superior to all its competitors, except perhaps the BMW 328, which was its equal. This enabled it to win most of the important rallies – the outstanding one being the best performance in the International Alpine Trial of 1936 – a performance which it repeated no less than 12 years later, in 1948, against all the very latest machinery. It also won first place in the R.A.C. Rally of 1937, and best overall performance and 1st in class in the Welsh Rally of the same year and again in 1938 and '39. These competition successes helped the company to build up a name for performance and things were going in the right direction, but I knew we had a long way to go before we were producing the type of car at which we were aiming.

3
46
RALLYE MONTE-CARLO
CVU 2

In 1935 my partner expressed a wish to retire. I investigated the possibility of making a public issue which yielded to the company £85,000. My partner took cash for his shares but I retained my 50% holding and later acquired additional shares to obtain a majority holding.

By March 1946 we issued £100,000 5½% Preference Shares of £1 each. Thus in total the finance introduced into the company since its inception amounted to £185,000.

Between 1955 and 1964 we issued to our shareholders bonus shares to the par value of £2,147,000 which, just prior to the amalgamation with B.M.C. to form B.M.H. had, together with the Ordinary and Preference Shares, a market value of £16m.

W
T4131

OPPOSITE Repairing Whitley bomber aircraft like this was an important war-time contract.
Photo: aviation-images.com/Mary Evans Picture Library

BELOW Daimler's Ferret armoured car would later become an unlikely Jaguar product.

War broke out in 1939 which, of course, put an end to car production and turned our energies to aircraft and aircraft engine components, for which we built up a sizeable machine shop. We made fuselages for Stirling bombers and the first Meteor jet fuselage – the Meteor was the first operational British jet aircraft to be produced. We repaired complete Whitley bombers, and manufactured a multitude of other things – including over 100,000 two-wheeled trailers.

I have a vivid recollection of the arrival of the first Whitley bombers at our Foleshill factory, as they went past my office window on a convoy of Queen Mary transporters. I followed them into the factory and was surprised how little they appeared to be damaged. Together with the works manager and chief inspector, I examined them carefully, and I made the remark to them – which I will never forget – "We'll have them repaired in under a month." Some of them were still there a year later. I was at the time ignorant of the stringent Aeronautical Inspection Directorate requirements. Each aircraft had to be stripped to the extent that its repair almost required the same number of man-hours as a complete aircraft. I still think that, at that critical time, some short-cuts should have been made in view of the urgent need to get them back into the air as quickly as possible, as there was so much risk involved in fighting the war and such an acute shortage of aircraft that this would have been a comparatively minor risk. Evidence of the very serious nature of the shortage of aircraft was brought forcibly to light by Lord Beaverbrook when he re-established the Whitley, which had been relegated to the reserve list, and cancelled the new Manchester aircraft, for which we had already built a new factory and partly equipped it with plant. We had looked forward to building the Manchester, but we threw ourselves wholeheartedly into getting the damaged Whitleys back into the air as quickly as we could. We were responsible not only for repairing them, but also for getting them flight tested and, for this purpose, we used a nearby airfield which had been commandeered for us.

One of the questions I have been asked many times is "Why did we choose the name 'Jaguar'?"

We felt that we should give a model name to the new 1936 O.H.V. models, so I asked our publicity people to let me have a list of the names of animals, fish and birds. I immediately pounced on 'Jaguar' for it had an exciting sound to me, and brought back some memories of the stories told to me, towards the end of the 1914-1918 war, by an old school friend who, being nearly a year older than I, had joined the Royal Flying Corps, as it was called in those days. He was stationed at Farnborough and he used to tell me of his work as a mechanic on the Armstrong Siddeley 'Jaguar' engine. Since that time, the word Jaguar has always had a particular significance to me and so S.S. 'Jaguar' became the name by which our cars were known.

WHP 205J

OPPOSITE Jaguar was happy to share its name with the BAC jet strike fighter, seen here chasing a V12 E-type Series III.

After the war the initials S.S. had acquired a tarnished image, as it was a reminder of the German S.S. troops, a sector of the community which was not highly regarded, and it was considered to be most desirable to discontinue its use and changed the name of the company from S.S. Cars Limited to Jaguar Cars Limited. Before we did this and in spite of our already having used the name, I asked Sir Frank Spriggs, then managing director of Armstrong Siddeley and with whom I had become friendly during the war, if he had any objections to our doing so. He said they had no intention of using the name and agreed to our proposal both verbally and in writing. It is amusing that some 23 years later the British Aircraft Corporation should ask our permission to call their new jet strike fighter 'Jaguar' – to which we agreed, but later we were unable to agree that their joint company with the French 'Breguet' Company should be formed under a title incorporating the Jaguar name. Our choice of name has proved to be most fortunate for it has helped to build up our world image. There are few places to which one can go where the name 'Jaguar' is not known as a car.

ABOVE Wielding the hand-welder on an E-type Series III in the factory in 1971.

OPPOSITE What's it worth? London launch of the first S.S. Jaguar in 1935 at a price that drew gasps.

OVERLEAF Brand new E-type Series Is filling the office car park at Browns Lane, with a preponderance of red, white and blue…

Some months before the end of the war,

in 1945, we received a 'go ahead' from the government that we might revert some of our activities to our peacetime production. Coincidental with this, John Black advised me that he intended to concentrate the whole of the Standard organisation on the production of one model which he was to call the 'Vanguard'. He told me that he would no longer be able to make our engine and, after some discussion, offered to sell to us the special plant he had put in for its production – very generously at the written-down value. Before the war, Black had given me reason for a great deal of anxiety on the question of the exclusive continuity of the engine he was making for us. Several other makers had asked him to supply them, and I had not found it easy to prevent him doing so, even though he accepted that the design of the engine, apart from the cylinder block and crankshaft, was ours. Therefore I was delighted to learn of his proposals as I felt it was a release from an arrangement which I could not have broken honourably, having regard for the fact that it was his willingness to put down the plant, which we could not afford at the time, that got us off the ground with this new engine. I saw this move as a great step towards our becoming the self-contained manufacturing unit at which I aimed.

E 141

JAGUAR

I had a great admiration for John Black in many respects, but I quickly grasped the opportunity to obtain security. Therefore, within a few days, I sent transport to collect the plant and sent our cheque in payment for it. It turned out that I had been right to do so for it was not long before Black proposed that he should revert back to the old arrangement and return the plant to Standard's. I said "No, thank you, John, I have now got the ball, and I would rather kick it myself." He pressed me very hard, even to the extent that we should form a separate company together, but I was unwilling to accept his proposals, even though I so much appreciated his help in the past.

About that time the Triumph Company,

which occupied an adjacent factory to ours, was in very 'low water' and a receiver named Graham was appointed. He approached me to ascertain if we were interested in purchasing the company. They had previously sold the motorcycle side of the business in the mistaken belief that it was this which was responsible for the losses. Jack Sangster, who had built up Ariel after it had gone into liquidation 20 years before, bought it and, I believe, had made £100,000 the first year, largely due to Edward Turner, who designed for him an entirely new machine. We examined the Triumph balance sheets and the prospects of the company and realised that, without jeopardising our resources, we would be unable to restore the company to a profit earning basis, and it would be better to concentrate on our own increasingly successful company.

ABOVE Jaguar Mk2 3.8-litre at Monza, Italy in 1963, where it covered 10,000 miles at a record-breaking average of 106.58mph.

OPPOSITE The powerhouse of Jaguar's post-war success was its acclaimed XK twin-cam six-cylinder engine.

JAGUAR

OPPOSITE Lyons looked at taking over Triumph, which made this Dolomite saloon in the late 1930s, but preferred to concentrate on Jaguar instead.

BELOW The racy XK 150 roadster when brand new, in a somewhat more sedate British setting.

The availability of Triumph brought Black back into the picture. He told me he had been going into the question of buying it, but he would not do so if I would change my mind and join forces with him. I told him I could not change my mind, whereupon he said he would buy Triumph and go into competition with us. He said he could not see us surviving it, and he did make some success of Triumph, but it did not have the effect upon us that he had forecast. In spite of our differences, I would like to pay tribute to him for his great energy and the success he made of the Standard Motor Company in the early post-war years.

OPPOSITE Test Driver Norman Dewis took this lightly modified XK 120 to a spectacular 172mph in 1953 at Jabbeke, Belgium.

With the end of the war in sight, we started thinking about our return to car production and decided that we must make the finest engine it was possible to design. Our research satisfied us that we must go for a twin overhead camshaft hemispherical head, six cylinder unit and we set our sights as high as we could. We had a first-class engine team headed by W. Hassan, under the direction of our Chief Engineer W.M. Heynes. In two years we produced an engine which had a far greater horse-power per litre than any other engine in the world which was available to the public as a normal production unit.

This new engine – the XK – put us right into the forefront and, in 1948, we introduced it in what was regarded as an entirely new conception of a sports car – the XK 120 – so christened because its estimated top speed was 120 m.p.h. This proved to be far below the car's capabilities for, when we took it to Belgium, together with a chartered 'plane-load of the Press, and demonstrated it on the Jabbeke autoroute, the car attained a speed of 132.59 miles per hour. This was a tremendous increase in speed compared with anything that had been achieved before by a standard production vehicle. It had been intended that the car would just be a test-bed for the new engine and the bodies were virtually hand-made in aluminium. However, so great was the demand that we went ahead with a pressed steel body for volume production.

CONTROLE
ROYAL AUTOMOBILE CLUB DE BELGIQUE
522.379

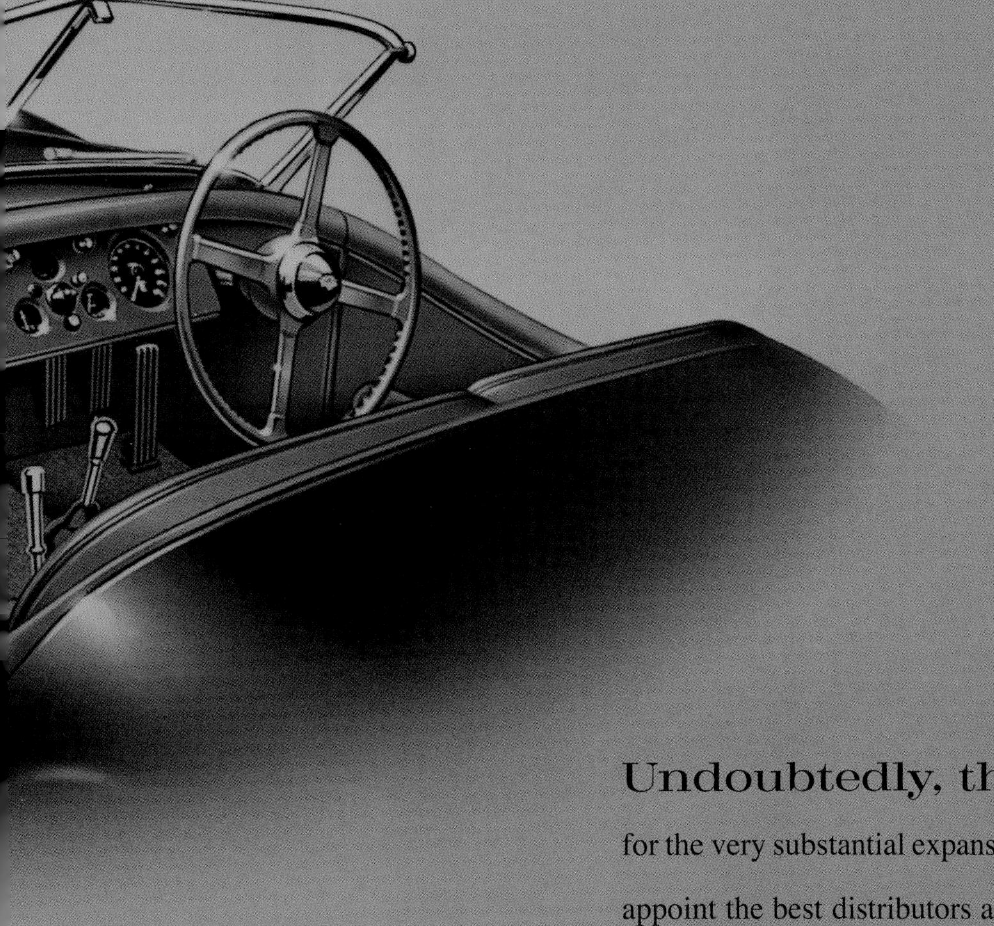

LEFT Illustrations from early Jaguar XK 120 sales material emphasising practical details and super-sleek lines.

Undoubtedly, this model paved the way

for the very substantial expansion of our American business and enabled us to appoint the best distributors and dealers available to us. Although they were in the main in a very small way of business, because no American franchise holder was permitted, nor indeed is he permitted today, to sell competitive makes, many of these distributors built up magnificent organisations largely due to the Jaguar business.

OPPOSITE Hand-finishing a Jaguar S-type shell at Browns Lane; assuring the supply of bodies was one reason that compelled Lyons to merge with BMC in 1966.

BELOW The Jaguar E-type Series III V12 guaranteed owner delight.

OVERLEAF Crowds around the Jaguar display at the 1970 New York Auto Show for the crucial US market.

One of the major problems facing us after the war was the rationing of steel. Permits were required and this provided a very limited allowance for home market business. We had enjoyed only a limited export market before the war, because we had always been able to sell on the domestic market all the cars we could make. So we did not go to the expense of establishing export outlets – a situation which would be very much criticised today. Accordingly, we set out to convince the government that the models we had coming along would command a substantial export market. We prepared a very elaborate brochure, which set out our programme for exports – the countries to which we were going to sell, the number of cars and the amount of steel we required. I delivered this personally to Sir George Turner, who was then Permanent Secretary to the Ministry of Supply, and I elaborated verbally on our plans and obtained the promise of support. Within two weeks we received a permit for the full quota of steel for which we had asked. This gave us a tremendous boost, because we only had to make the cars for selling which was no problem in the car-starved world. However, we did not allow this to lead us into a state of false security. We went flat-out to establish selling outlets throughout the world which enabled us to reach one of the highest – if not the highest – percentage of export sales in the industry. At one time, nearly 80% of our cars were going abroad and we have rarely – if ever – dropped below 50%.

RENAULT
RENAULT
RENAULT 10 SIERRA
1960

RENAULT
BRITISH LEYLAND
BRITISH LEYLAND

LEFT The XK 120 in its pure original form, the left-hand drive here a signifier of its importance to Jaguar's exports.

A very good example of the progress we made, apart from North America, was the establishment of a new distributor in Australia. The distributor who, in a half-hearted way, had represented us before the war was not disposed to contract with us for more than 100 cars per year, and we had much more ambitious plans. It became known in Australia that we were prepared to change our distributor and, in consequence, we received a cable from a then comparatively small dealer, Bryson Motors, offering to contract for 2,000 cars in the first year, if we would appoint him as our distributor. We obtained excellent references, although they only represented Morgan, and a number of motor-cycle companies. We made the appointment and it was only because we could not supply them with the full 2,000 cars that they did not reach this target. In fact, they did exceed 1,500. Within two years, this distributor had taken over the showrooms of our previous distributor, which were the finest in Sydney, and have never failed to take the cars for which they have contracted.

I think I can fairly claim that Jaguar and MG virtually pioneered the U.S.A. market for imported cars, which now represents some 10% of vehicle sales. Volkswagen have by far the largest share of this business. It is interesting to recall that, in those early days, they proved very difficult to sell. So much so, in fact, that the then distributor for the East Coast, who was also the distributor of Volkswagen for the whole of the U.S.A., insisted that all dealers who ordered a Jaguar had to take two Volkswagens as well!

ABOVE Jaguar XK 150 drophead coupé.

OPPOSITE Lyons ensured racing was always linked to the production cars in Jaguar marketing; indeed, the engine in both D-type and Mk VII was fundamentally identical.

APRIL 20, 1955

The Motor

EVERY WEDNESDAY
ONE SHILLING

The finest car of its class in the world

JAGUAR

20
153 RW

The XK 120 was tremendously success- ful in sports car races in all parts of the world and it was as a result of Leslie Johnson and Bert Hadley's outstanding performance with one of these cars in the 1950 Le Mans race, in which they succeeded in getting into third position in the last few hours of the race, before they retired with a broken clutch, that we decided that, in a car more suitable for the race, the XK engine could win this greatest of all events. So, in 1951 we arrived at Le Mans with a brand new team of three C-types in charge of F.R.W. England as competition manager, who later became joint managing director and, in January this year, deputy chairman. It was immediately obvious from the practice sessions that these cars could outpace the competition and this proved to be the case in the race itself. Stirling Moss and Jack Fairman led for about 8 hours, until they fell out with loss of oil pressure due to the failure of an oil pipe flange. Unfortunately, the same fate befell Leslie Johnson and Clemente Biondetti, but Peter Whitehead and Peter Walker went on to win at a record speed for the race. It was the first time that a British car had won at Le Mans since 1935, that is for 15 years. This success set a pattern which we were to follow and improve upon during the next eight years. Jaguar finished in 1st place at Le Mans on five occasions, 1st and 2nd place on two occasions, and on another occasion – 1st, 2nd, 3rd and 4th places.

OPPOSITE Spaceframe chassis, an aerodynamic shape and disc brakes turned the C-type into Jaguar's first Le Mans winner.

ABOVE Duncan Hamilton (left) and Tony Rolt celebrate their Jaguar C-type 24-hour victory at Le Mans in 1953.

The reliability and performance of the XK engine had been proved in the XK 120 and it was, therefore, with every confidence that we put it into a new saloon, the Mk VII, which was to be announced at the 1950 Earls Court Motor Show. *The Autocar* described it as the 'Prima Ballerina of the Show'.

OPPOSITE Daimler's factory at Radford, Coventry (shown during a 1940s Royal visit) was acquired in 1960, allowing Jaguar massive expansion.

BELOW Stirling Moss and Norman Dewis in the Jaguar C-type on the 1953 Mille Miglia course.

By 1951 our production had again outgrown the capacity of our factory and the need for expansion was vital to our continued progress, but we were faced with a particularly difficult position because, although I went to the highest level, we were unable to obtain permission to extend our factory; there was a complete embargo on building in Coventry. At that time a shadow factory in Browns Lane, Coventry, which was occupied by Daimler, was falling into disuse, as Daimler's were moving back into their Radford factory. After many hours of talks with the 'powers that be', I was able to purchase the Browns Lane factory – the only shadow factory, I believe even today, not on a rental basis. There was one condition – that we should undertake the manufacture of the Rolls-Royce 'Meteor' tank engine, which was required to meet the rearmament programme at that time. We tooled up this magnificent engine and had it in production within two years, well ahead of the programme date. Although we were very proud of this achievement, we were pleased when the contract suddenly came to an end, so enabling us to step-up car production, which was beginning to be adversely affected.

In 1955 we introduced the first of a completely new range of medium size saloon cars which was to form the basis for a steady increase in our production. This 2.4 litre saloon was followed by the 3.4 litre and then, in 1959 in revised Mark 2 form with the addition of the 3.8 litre engine. Subsequent models carried the titles 'S' type and 420 – the latter featuring our big 4.2 litre engine. This range of models accounted for a substantial increase, not only in our volume of production, but also in our profits, which rose five-fold between 1955 and 1968.

ABOVE The 1959 Mk2 quickly became a potent emblem of personal achievement.

OPPOSITE The 1955 2.4-litre, first of Jaguar's compact sports saloons.

LEFT Aftermath of the 1957 factory fire… but 'backs to the wall' team spirit saw normal production resumed in just six weeks. *Photo: Alamy*

OVERLEAF Sir William Lyons and his wonderfully diverse portfolio of products at Browns Lane, Coventry in May 1962. *Photo: Mirrorpix*

In 1957 we had a disastrous fire in which we lost nearly half our main factory. It appeared that it would be impossible for us to produce cars for many months, but the misfortune acted like magic on our workpeople, suppliers, building contractors and fellow manufacturers. We were inundated with offers of help, loan of plant, personnel – in fact anything we could ask for. Our workpeople 'buckled-to', offering to work, for day-rate pay, with shovels and anything they could lay their hands on to clear up the mess.

Our building contractors brought in many of their competitors and the task of rebuilding was started within 48 hours of the fire. Tarpaulin structures were erected to provide temporary working protection and, in exactly nine days, production on a limited scale had recommenced, and within six weeks we were back to normal. It was a wonderful experience and another example of what the people of this country can do when they have their 'backs to the wall'.

By 1960 our factory was once again

'bursting at the seams'. Unfortunately, this came just at the time when the Government was increasing its pressure on manufacturers who wished to expand, to move into distressed areas and, of course, no factory extensions were permitted in Coventry. It came to my knowledge that the Daimler Company, which occupied the very fine factory at Radford, within two miles of our existing factory at Browns lane, was for sale. After some preliminary talks with Jack Sangster, who was then the chairman of B.S.A., having followed Sir Bernard Docker, we eventually agreed terms for us to acquire the Daimler Company. I do not recall a more amicable deal with anyone although, when we both thought everything had been settled, a matter of £10,000 arose between us. Since each of us was honestly convinced that this was in our own favour, we decided that the only way to settle the matter was to toss-up for it. I am pleased to say that I won.

GUAR
Better Flavour!
Ty·Phoo Tea
Mobilgas
280 EKC

V8 250

OPPOSITE Inspired union of Jaguar Mk2 body and Daimler SP250's 2.5-litre V8 engine produced the popular Daimler V8 250 luxury saloon.

BELOW Early example of the Daimler Fleetline bus.

The Daimler factory just about doubled our floor space and, in addition, we acquired a bus manufacturing company as well as a contract from the Government for the Daimler Ferret armoured fighting vehicle. Both were at a very low ebb – the output of buses being no more than three per week and the orders for Ferret showing a decline. In spite of the diminishing Government contracts for the Ferret when we took over, so good is the vehicle that it has not yet been replaced, and we have continued to make it in limited numbers. Indeed, it is one of the standard wheeled vehicles for NATO forces.

An unfortunate inheritance which we also acquired with Daimler was the run-down state of the car side of the business. The number of cars they had been making had fallen so low that it required a completely new approach to the whole question of volume, type and price. We resolved the problem by introducing the excellent Daimler 2½ litre V8 engine into our Mark 2 body shell and it proved to be a very good selling car indeed. We also followed this policy of using volume production bodies and units to produce the Daimler Sovereign – a car which has gained a very high reputation.

ABOVE The Guy Big J (for Jaguar, naturally) truck range was developed after Lyons rescued Guy Motors with a cheeky offer.

OPPOSITE Brochure artwork for the 1966 Daimler Sovereign, a lightly restyled Jaguar 420.

There were some good engineers at Daimler under the leadership of C.M. Simpson, and it was not long before we brought out the 'Fleetline' double deck bus chassis, which had a very good reception from municipal and national authorities, and now enjoys a very high reputation. In fact, in 1968, Daimler produced more rear-engined double deck bus chassis than any other manufacturer.

Entry into the bus market also provided us with an opportunity to get into the heavy commercial vehicle industry, so we set up a small engineering department at Daimler, under a very competent designer – C. Elliot – who had been responsible for the highly successful Dodge truck. However, before the final design was completed, I learned that a receiver had been appointed at Guy Motors Ltd. of Wolverhampton by Lloyds Bank and I saw this as an opportunity to speed-up our entry into the commercial vehicle field. Guy Motors was a long established firm, with a reputation for producing quality vehicles, but I must say that a visit to the factory had some discouraging effects, and the balance sheets of the company showed that they had been making losses over

THE DAIMLER
Sovereign

DAILY
DOLPHIN
SHOWS
BATTERSEA
FUN FAIR
Shepherds Bush
Hammersmith Putney
Wandsworth Garratt La
220
HARROW ROAD
DAILY
DOLPHIN
SHOWS
BATTERSEA
FUN FAIR
EGP 73 J

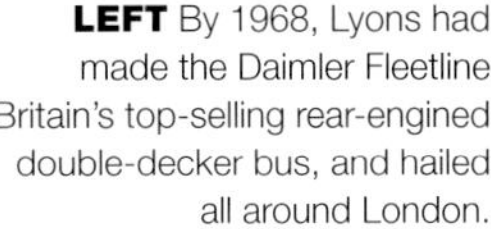

LEFT By 1968, Lyons had made the Daimler Fleetline Britain's top-selling rear-engined double-decker bus, and hailed all around London.

the previous four years at an average of nearly £300,000 per annum. I had long negotiations with the receiver and, eventually, made him an offer. I made it clear that, whilst I appreciated it was a low offer, it was the maximum to which I was prepared to go. He put this offer to the bank and they accepted it.

We transferred the small commercial vehicle engineering department from Daimler to Guy, reorganised the administration, and put the general manager, Arthur Jones, in charge as managing director. Only three years later we introduced a completely new range of heavy duty quality trucks known as the Guy Big J range. We put a lot of effort and 'know how' into Guy and we were soon out of the loss making situation and profits have built up to over £300,000 per annum. I am sure that Guy will play an important part in the future of the BLMC Bus and Truck division.

ABOVE Shining examples – Mk2s flowing off the Coventry assembly line in about 1962.

OPPOSITE Green-lit by Lyons in the mid-1960s, Jaguar's superb V12 engine made its debut in a revised E-type in 1971, a year before the founder officially retired.

In 1963 we acquired Coventry Climax.

We had a great admiration for their achievements and Mr. Leonard Lee had built up a most successful fork lift truck and fire pump business. The story of how the fire pump engine was developed into a successful racing car engine is, I believe, well-known. It is not so generally known, except in racing circles, that this engine, together with its successors, which completely dominated Grand Prix racing during the whole of the period during which the company participated in racing, was masterminded by Leonard Lee and executed by Walter Hassan, who had earlier left Jaguar to become chief engineer at Coventry Climax. He had left with our goodwill but we were pleased that he rejoined us as a result of this acquisition. Walter Hassan is now Group Chief Engineer (Power Units) heading a team which, I think it is generally recognised, is one of the most able in the country.

JAGUAR

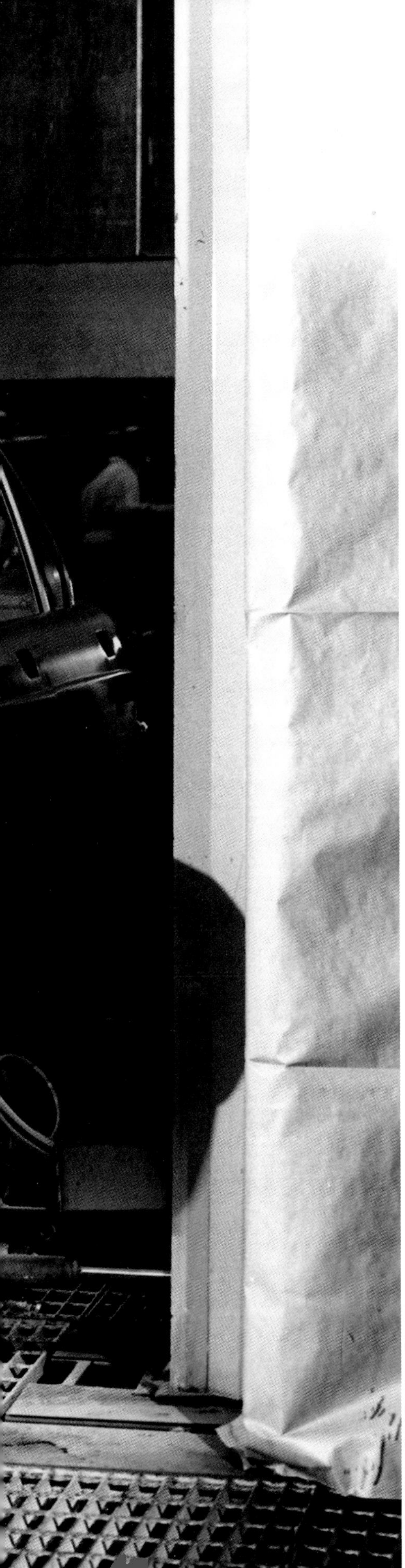

LEFT An XJ Series III bodyshell passing through the Castle Bromwich paintshop in the 1980s, after significant investment had greatly improved quality.

OVERLEAF The XJ-S grand tourer of 1975, seen here in its purest original form, was the final Jaguar fully envisioned under Sir William's watchful eye.

Finally, in 1964, we bought Henry Meadows, Wolverhampton. Apart from their light engineering interests, they also manufactured an excellent range of marine gearboxes.

In these six factories we employ approximately 10,000 persons; in addition to cars, we produce trucks, buses, coaches, material handling equipment, fire pumps, marine gearboxes and armoured fighting vehicles. We export over 50% of our car output – one of the highest percentage of exports in total production in the industry – and we have active trade relations with over 104 different countries.

GJW 253W

RIGHT One-piece curved windscreen and two-tone paint identify the MkVIII of 1956.

In the mid 60s there was talk about the leading British manufacturers getting together so that as an industry we would better be able to face world competition. I was an enthusiastic protagonist as I believed that this was both necessary and desirable. We had many discussions together, but marriages of this kind are not easily arranged and little progress was made until Sir George Harriman said to me one day "We don't seem to be making much progress, what about you and I getting together?" I agreed, although I knew this would mean having to give up my majority holding in the organisation I had founded, and British Motor Holdings Limited was the outcome. This was soon followed by Rover joining Leyland. I played an active role in the negotiations which, in May 1968, completed the unification of 95% of the British motor industry, under the banner of the British Leyland Motor Corporation, now headed by Lord Stokes, thus creating the second largest motor group outside America.

All this is a far cry from the three men and a boy with which this story began.

JAGUAR

LEFT The Jaguar XK 140 roadster.

Exciting as it all has been, the main objective of a business is to make profits and our record in this respect has been one of the best in the industry. Nevertheless, in the last few years, the growth of the company and the return on capital employed has been adversely affected by the many production delays resulting from strike action in our own factories and those of our suppliers. These stoppages are such a prominent feature of our activities today and occupy so much of the time of our senior management that I cannot omit making reference to our labour relations. I hold very strong views that, in the present conditions prevailing in our factories, which provide wide-open opportunities for our workpeople to support, by unconstitutional strike action, any demands they may care to make, we will never be able to achieve the standard of efficiency necessary for us to compete on a level with other countries. I do not subscribe to the oft-repeated statement that we compare favourably with other countries in the man hours we lose through unofficial strikes. If this were true our competitors would be suffering production delays similar to our own and there is certainly no evidence that this is the case. I can see no sensible reason why agreements, freely entered into, between employers and unions should not be

BELOW E-type and a twisting cross-country road – a scenario on which the classic car obsession was founded.

OPPOSITE Getaway car? Not many '60s villains could outrun an expertly conducted Mk2…

binding in law. I do not accept that the unions cannot exercise disciplinary authority over their members; there is substantial evidence that they do not hesitate to do so when any of their members depart from the unions' own rules. I believe that the unions must face up to their responsibilities not to their members alone, but to British industry and the country as a whole. I welcome the determination of the present Government to take some positive, immediate, and effective steps to rectify this disgraceful situation which so often has completely blocked Britain's road to economic recovery.

I do not believe that, as presented, the Government's plans will have the desired effect – indeed, certain aspects of the proposals could well increase the problems from which we suffer in achieving efficient productivity within our factories.

No history of Jaguar would be complete without reference to the important part which has been played by our distributors and dealers at home and overseas for, without their loyal support, we could never have achieved the rate of progress of the past 46 years. During this, we have made many good friends and established some very close relationships. Our close relationships, in particular, have anticipated the

Boy's Own
PAPER
NOVEMBER
1962
PRICE
ONE SHILLING

In this issue
Training the Z CAR MEN
by Charles Fothergill

JAGUAR

OPPOSITE Lyons' masterpiece, the XJ6, was finding its first excited customers as he delivered this address.

BELOW A 4.2-litre XK engine gave the XJ6 its journey-shrinking stride, although a smaller 2.8 was also offered.

period of great change through which we are now passing, in which the dependence of the retailer on the manufacturer and vice versa is emerging as a major factor. Competition is increasing in severity with each year that goes by and, as a result, a really sound retail organisation is fast becoming one of the most vital aspects of a manufacturer's expansion. Conversely, retailers are increasingly dependent on the products of one manufacturer – or one group of manufacturers – and their success or failure is now largely based on each other's performance.

Equally important, we have been able to establish a very close relationship with our suppliers, not only through the normal course of business, but also through the various joint development projects we have undertaken to develop new materials and ideas. In today's conditions, the supplier has an unenviable role in that he must base his development upon the expansion plans of the industry which, however firmly and realistically based, so often founder in the quicksands of Government financial and economic planning. Until the government cease to use the motor industry as an economic regulator, and until we are able to eliminate unconstitutional strikes, I can see little hope of the industry as a whole making the type of progress which modern conditions demand.

ROLE OF THE SPECIALIST CAR

I have often been asked how Jaguar manage to produce their cars at such competitive prices. We have irrefutable evidence that the enquirers also accept that they represent good value and, in reality, we are striving to achieve both targets – good value and competitive prices. The answer lies in what I would term a straightforward business approach – firstly, the design and development of a product capable of generating a high consumer demand, secondly, the manufacturing of the product in volume and in the most economic way and, thirdly, the provision of a good follow-up service. I would add that, in Jaguar, we have always tried to run our organisation as economically as possible and to purchase our components at the best possible price consistent with the standards of quality. Above all, we have concentrated exclusively on a specific sector of the car market and aimed at providing complete coverage of that sector through a combination of models produced in quantity. Over the years, this has enabled us to justify the expenditure of very large sums of money indeed, in terms of machinery and tooling, knowing that the products of this investment could be utilised in several different models. The XK engine is a good example of our philosophy.

PREVIOUS PAGE Test driver Norman Dewis and the prototype Jaguar XJ13.

OPPOSITE Ian Appleyard's Jaguar MkVII on the 1953 Monte Carlo Rally, when he came a strong second overall.

Introduced in 1948, it is still at least the equal of any power unit available today – and the very considerable cost of tooling it up for volume production has been justified many times over. I would add that, in decisions of this magnitude, one has to have complete faith in one's own judgement – had we taken the advice of the respected authorities of the time we would not have gone ahead with the project. Similarly, had it failed, I doubt very much whether Jaguar would have been in the progressive situation it is in today.

You may be surprised to hear that, in my opinion, the main pressures on the specialist car manufacturers are coming from below – from the volume car producers – rather than from other competitors in the specialist field. Until a few years ago the type of car produced by the specialists was out of reach of the volume producers – they did not possess the people, facilities, know-how or attitudes, all of which are essential ingredients for a specialist car. I am not being smug in making this assertion – it is not too difficult to think of volume producers, on both sides of the Atlantic, who have tried to produce a specialist luxury car and fallen well short of even their initial production targets. I admit that the converse could be equally true. Today, the situation is very different and the high volume producers are achieving a standard of refinement and luxury which would have been unattainable only a few years ago.

MARCH 15, 1961
The Motor
EVERY WEDNESDAY
ONE SHILLING
Full details in this issue
The most advanced sports car
in the world....
JAGUAR 'E' TYPE
Grand Touring Models

In the past, one could safely describe a specialist car as one which offered particularly high standards of design, manufacture and performance – with an emphasis also on quality and luxury, particularly if it were a saloon or convertible. These attributes – singly or collectively – appealed to the connoisseurs of motoring who were invariably prepared to pay a considerable premium for such vehicles. Generally speaking, it was produced in small quantities, and many of the best-known names of pre-World War Two days were manufacturers of this type. Unhappily, the fact that so few survive today is an indication of the fierceness of the competition with which we are having to contend. Into this select group, we injected the Jaguar models – different in design and appearance and with a good performance but produced in relatively large volumes in order to make the price realistic. I believe that, in those now far-off days, we started a whole new approach to specialist cars, and one which is now expanding rapidly.

OPPOSITE Announcing the E-type in no uncertain terms in March 1961.

ABOVE The E-type arrives in Geneva for its worldwide unveiling.

RIGHT After a 1-2-3 finish at Le Mans in 1953, the victorious Jaguar C-types and their drivers enjoyed a jubilant civic reception back home in Coventry.

Since the war, the position has changed

considerably and with increasing rapidity – particularly in the past eight or ten years. The pent-up demand for cars, resulting from the war years, has been totally dissipated and the output of the major manufacturers, particularly in the U.S.A. and Europe, has raced ahead. In the U.S.A., for example, 1960 sales totalled 6.5 million, in 1968 they reached 9.5 million – an increase of 50%. A large percentage of this increase can be attributed to two main factors – the increasing affluence of the American car-buying public and, more recently, the appearance of a new interpretation of the specialist car – the 'personalised' car. This approach has opened up a completely new sector of the market and one with great and growing potential. In my view, it is complementary to the established specialist and luxury car concepts. In the three-year period since 1966, luxury cars in the U.S.A. increased their sales to 386,000 units or 4.5% of total production. But in 1964, the first of the new generation of personalised cars was launched – that phenomenon of the U.S.A. market – the Ford Mustang.

OUTFITTERS
NO ENTRY
17

MGF 328
TC.233-Aug 92.

OPPOSITE The Jaguar MkV drophead coupé of 1948, fitting its owners to a tee.

BELOW Bertone's 1967 Pirana reinterpretation of the Jaguar E-type, a possible pointer to the specialist car of the 1970s.

Since then, others have followed with exotic names such as Camaro, Firebird, Cougar, A.M.X. Javelin, Charger, etc, all of which offer a stylish and sporting approach to motoring. In the past three years, the battle has been staged between no less than 12 individual models and these alone sold over one million units in 1968 or 11% of total sales. The very lengthy list of options ranging from four or five different engine capacities and power outputs, wide and close-ratio gearboxes, several different types of wheels – even down to bonnet-mounted revolution counters, enable each and every purchaser to build his own particular version of the car. For example, over 86% of purchasers in 1968 chose one or other of the optional V8 engines, 41% ordered air conditioning, and 33% padded roofs. Who is to say that cars of this type are not the modern equivalent of the specialist car of earlier days? Certainly not me. They may not represent a thoroughbred version of a specialist car – particularly in terms of engineering design – but they do provide cars which are different and which offer a particular type of motoring.

RIGHT Individual and striking: the Daimler Double Six in its 1931 form (background) and recreated by Jaguar in 1974.

One of the strengths of the specialist car manufacturer used to lie in his ability to provide exactly what the customer required. The large volume producer completely lacked this flexibility – the Henry Ford axiom of "any colour, as long as it's black" was all too true. Today, everything has changed. The immense resources of the largest manufacturers and the use of computers for production and stock control, enable the giants to offer a staggering variety of options at extremely competitive prices and, as I have described, to sell them in very large volume.

A similar pattern is emerging in Europe, but in a different form. The optional equipment list is very much shorter, but some of Europe's largest manufacturers are producing, in quantity, either luxury and/or high performance versions of their normal production cars or complete specialist-type cars with individual and very striking bodywork. The effect is still the same in that an increasing number of motorists in Europe and America are able to sample a form of motoring which, only a few years ago, was quite out of their reach. The tremendous success of the 'E' Type reflects the worldwide enthusiasm which exists for these types of car – particularly in America. Production of the 'E' Type is running at a record level and 95% is exported to the USA market alone.

HHP 7M

OPPOSITE Testing an early E-type roadster at the Motor Industry Research Association's high-speed track in Nuneaton, Warwickshire.

BELOW Mk2 saloons made excellent competition cars in saloon racing, with ample power and a chassis fine-tuned for high-speed handling

In the context of this somewhat awesome situation what action can a specialist manufacturer take to protect his interests? Firstly, I believe that he too must ensure that he keeps in step with the rapid advances in production technology, to ensure a competitive unit cost. Secondly, he must be prepared to change the style and design of his cars more frequently than in the past. Thirdly, and most important of all he must offer qualities which just cannot be provided by the giants. The car must possess very high standards of refinement, silence, handling and comfort to give to its owner that indefinable sense of satisfaction. Here I refer to the need to employ truly advanced standards of engineering concepts and design – he must always try to be first with any new development – and he must also offer the highest standards of quality, not only in terms of material but also in terms of

BELOW XJ6 prototype undergoing pre-production road testing.

OPPOSITE E-type prototype called E1A, clearly showing its D-type racing car influence.

assembly and overall product reliability. For example, before the war, Jaguar were the first to offer a heating and ventilating system as part of the standard specification and to produce a true flush-fitting sliding roof. Since the war we have pioneered the use of disc brakes and high-speed tyres for normal road use – both of these in conjunction with the Dunlop Rubber Company – and the use of fully automatic transmission as standard equipment in a British car. Fourthly, by the judicious use of the right type of promotion, he must endow his products with that aura of 'exclusiveness' which is the hallmark of the true specialist car. A manufacturer cannot be far off the mark if it is the ambition of every keen motorist to own one of his cars. Such a situation exists with the XJ6 which even at this early stage in its life is destined, not only to increase the prestige of Jaguar, but also to further advance the success of the company as a whole.

VKV752

OPPOSITE The Ron Flockhart/ Ivor Bueb D-type on its way to winning the 24 Hours of Le Mans, Jaguar's fifth victory there, in 1957.

BELOW Formula 1 hero Graham Hill gave this car the E-type's first race win in 1961.

OVERLEAF A successor to the E-type in every sense: the F-type sports car.

It may be thought that the extremely competitive situation in the world's motor industry is the beginning of the end for the specialist car manufacturer. In my view, nothing could be further from the truth. Our experience to date indicates that the interest being shown by the big manufacturers in specialised types of cars is, in fact, doing a valuable job of work for companies such as Jaguar, by building up a very large group of motorists who, having acquired a liking for a car which is different, are only two anxious to widen the experience by the purchase of a true specialist car.

We live in an era of mass production and increasing standardisation. I believe that these conditions are ideal for the growth of the specialist car manufacturer. It is our job to ensure that when the motorist finally tires of the offerings of the big producers, we are ready and waiting to seize the opportunity. We, in Jaguar, intend to go on doing just that!

COMMENTARY

By Giles Chapman

BELOW INSET Wappenbury with the Jaguar range in 1985, the year of Sir William's sad passing aged 83.

Sir William Lyons

delivered the very personal account of how he created Jaguar – reproduced over the previous pages – in April 1969, to an assembled audience of motor industry leaders in London. Some of it can be heard online in a scratchy and incomplete tape recording, and his delivery is anything but booming. He's quietly-spoken and sometimes stumbles over names, but there's a calmness to the way he tells his story that is curiously reassuring. The man instigated and carried out absolutely everything he describes, and the matter-of-factness of his immense achievements is one of the most extraordinary things about this material.

For 34 years, at that point, people had loved choosing and driving a Jaguar, and many would have been aware of the make's five wins in the 24 Hours of Le Mans endurance race. Mostly, they wouldn't have known anything at all about William Lyons, much less that a Jaguar E-type or Mk2 had connections with making motorbike sidecars in a wind-swept Blackpool backstreet. In 1969 the catalogue of written Jaguar history was still quite small; the classic car movement didn't yet exist, and the vintage car community were still in the habit of demeaning Jaguar for its homespun roots… and for the fact that its meteoric rise drove quite a few of their cherished marques into oblivion.

The British public, though, had recently become much more alert to Sir William. When the XJ6 was launched in September 1968, his benign and avuncular face had appeared in press advertisements to launch the car, not just in motoring magazines but also the powerful Sunday newspapers. It was an absolute first for the Jaguar founder, and he was reportedly reluctant to do so but, considering the importance of the new car, he agreed. At the time he addressed the IMI, XJ6 customer deliveries were gathering momentum, and the company was into its third month of working night shifts (having never done so before) to meet the tremendous demand. The car's excellence was being recognised by accolades such as *Car* magazine's Car Of The Year award and the Don Safety Trophy. Sir William was sometimes seen clutching the silverware, looking a bit bashful. Then in October 1969 he even featured in the TV commercial to launch the luscious new Daimler Sovereign.

TOP The Jaguar XJ-S in 1994 after several revamps that kept it selling strongly.

ABOVE An XJ-S V12 Cabriolet receives its finishing touches on the Browns Lane production line.

OPPOSITE Lyons' design process in action: working up early ideas for the XJ6, using a full-size mock-up, painted metal panels, and natural outdoor light.

Finally, here was the personification of all that was Jaguar. Mr Jaguar.

It is fascinating to see how, in his speech, Sir William puts such a light touch on the major event that has just taken place in his world: his loss, finally, of independence. In his version of events here, it's almost a casual suggestion by Sir George Harriman that leads to Jaguar and the British Motor Corporation (BMC) merging to 'better face world competition'. He avoids mention of the fact that in 1965 BMC had bought Pressed Steel Fisher, supplier of Jaguar's car bodies, and that he had little choice but to throw his lot in with a rival. You can easily detect this was not his natural instinct.

Then Jaguar's place within British Leyland was delicately negotiated so that Sir William had the maximum possible autonomy, while also retaining the clout to have potential rival products within the group – a Rolls-Royce-engined Austin-Healey, a mid-engined Rover sports car, a Vanden Plas luxury edition of the Austin 3-litre – all eliminated. His tactics were masterful, and paved the way for the launch in 1972 of the pinnacle to everything he'd built: the Jaguar XJ12, the world's first truly mass-produced V12 car.

In March 1972 Sir William, then aged 71, retired from Jaguar. His frustration at the industrial unrest he refers to in his address must surely have peaked shortly before he departed. In January that year 100 machinists working at the Radford engine plant had downed tools in just the latest of many disputes, and the two-week standstill added delay to launching the XJ12.

He had an imposing home at Wappenbury Hall near Leamington Spa, and a farm next door where he bred Suffolk sheep and Jersey cattle. His adoring wife – Lady Greta Lyons – would no doubt have appreciated some quality time with her husband away from 'The Jaguar'. They had a seaside holiday home in Devon too so, overall, quitting his office for relaxation should have been an attractive prospect; he enjoyed playing golf, gardening, and his pet dogs. Somehow, though, it seemed there was still unfinished business. What is not generally appreciated is that, until 1966, the money in Jaguar was largely Sir William's own. Everything he did was almost a personal risk. He had operated with thrift and discipline, aided by opportunistic purchases of secondhand equipment that would do the job and make parts of his operation last longer than they might have otherwise. The paint shop at Jaguar's Browns Lane, Coventry factory, for example, had been working flat-out for 20 years since 1950, but Sir William didn't have the resources for a new one, and it became an increasing source of frustration – for restive workers as much as grumpy management.

Hopes that British Leyland would provide the badly needed investment to produce Mercedes-beating cars quickly faded. For the founding father of Jaguar, the deteriorating state of his unique company must have hurt deeply. And something else that irked him enormously was – through British Leyland's malaise – the brake put on Jaguar's technological future. Sir William was characterised by never standing still on development. Under his driving leadership, Jaguars didn't stay in production long enough to become 'traditional'; he tended to look towards the horizon, and over it.

37

The adventurous XJ-S was the last car fully conceived under his watch, and like many Jaguars before it shocked the stick-in-the-muds and did things differently – it was a car like no other, deliberately different to, and even more sophisticated than, the E-type. Lyons just loved to move on. As he was saying his courteous goodbyes to colleagues in 1972, he knew his design and engineering team had already started work on the next Jaguar saloon range. He couldn't have comprehended that the car would not emerge until 1986 as the XJ40 series! By that time, Jaguar's existing cars were virtually living antiques, and Sir William would never have tolerated that…

In fact, behind the scenes, Lyons didn't let go entirely. Loyal staff would often greet him in and around Browns Lane, as he was known to 'pop in' almost weekly. One can only imagine the self-imposed agony as he witnessed quality levels plummet and dilapidation set in around the buildings and facilities. For this most dynamically entrepreneurial of Britain's car company bosses it must also have felt positively absurd that, in 1975, Jaguar Cars Ltd fell under state ownership, after the government stepped in to rescue British Leyland by nationalising it.

It was not recorded what Sir William thought of the XJ Series III in 1979. While he must have been heartened to see at least something new for the weary distributors and dealers – many of whom, as he relates in the address, he had personally appointed and set enormous store by – it was surely tempered by the fact that the design work had been handled by an outsider, Pininfarina. Jaguar not designing its own cars? Unthinkable. While he famously had no design training whatsoever, Sir William had personally refined the shapes of all the cars bearing the Jaguar name. Certainly not with a computer, and not much even with paper and pencils, but by working outside in natural light with full-size, three-dimensional mock-ups. He was helped by fast-working panelbeaters and his own uncanny eye – standing back, walking round, contemplating – as he made his magic.

The darkest hour is often before the dawn. And in July 1980 a little grey daylight started to play around the scruffy eaves of the Jaguar plant. With the shortlived and ineffective Jaguar-Rover-Triumph division of British Leyland dissolved, Jaguar Cars Ltd regained meaningful independence, and John Egan arrived as new chairman and chief executive. With a stellar track record in manufacturing, Egan only agreed to take on the basket case of Jaguar and turn it around if the company was a totally separate entity from the rest of British Leyland, and he could have complete autonomy.

It quickly turned into a crusade against poor processes and shoddy components that blighted the finished cars, and within two months seven of the 20 most pressing issues had been sorted out. Just making the windscreen and doors fit properly on the XJ, Egan told this author, saved the company £20m. "We did it with the enthusiasm and support of the workforce. I wondered what people had been doing all these years. It was mystifying." Egan would regularly pick a car off the production line and drive it home, returning the following morning and triggering

OPPOSITE John Egan (left) and Sir William Lyons, who enjoyed an excellent relationship in the first half of the 1980s.

TOP The XJ Series III sold strongly until ending production in 1992.

ABOVE The X300 series of XJ saloons (this is an XJ Sport) were faithfully evolved from the Lyons-era cars.

an "action day" to sort something out that he found wanting. "The chief executive today won't need to concern himself with things like this," Egan said, "but I did then. It was me saying yes, we can do all this stuff. When I saw the Pininfarina-facelifted XJ6, I knew that car could sell… if we could just make it work. Other British-made cars had faults too, so Jaguar wasn't unique, just a lot worse."

One of the very first things John Egan did, before all of this, was to contact Sir William. Never a hesitant character, Egan may still have been apprehensive when he suggested he'd love the Jaguar founder to return in the role of honorary president. With typical under-statement, Sr William replied: "Very kind of you but, actually, I already am.' Egan was shocked that, despite the senior position which should have funneled valuable elder-statesman wisdom into Jaguar's activities, he'd been almost completely ignored for five years.

That changed immediately. As Egan transformed the cars' quality, revived the XJ-S and took it racing, rebuilt US exports, pushed the XJ40 towards launch, and did everything humanly possible to make the Browns Lane plant more productive, Sir William was briefed and consulted every step of the way.

"He was very, very happy that the thing was beginning to look as though it was going to survive," Egan recalled. "He was a joy to work with. I could puzzle things out with Bill. I had a very rough relationship with the rest of BL, so it was nice to have someone like that who wasn't trying to kick me in the balls all the time!"

Although it was naturally very sad that Sir William Lyons died on 8 February, 1985 aged 83, he did so a happy man having seen his Jaguar Cars assuredly back on the road to success. This, of course, was boosted by an August 1984 return to the private sector in a stock market flotation. The allure of the Jaguar name was much easier for the public to grasp than a regional water board, and the level of interest was enormous. Applications for the 177,880,000 shares were 8.3 times oversubscribed. Jaguar Cars PLC was valued at £294m, and joined the FTSE Index as one of the UK's 100 biggest public companies.

Sir William's passing 50 years after the Jaguar name first appeared will soon mark the mid-point in the brand's history. It's journeyed an awfully long way since 1985 on its own.

The second half of the 1980s, despite the jubilation of its renaissance, brought a realisation that Jaguar's long-term independ-ence was unrealistic. After six years of valiantly going it alone, Ford bought the company in February 1990, the deal valuing Jaguar at a staggering £1.65bn. Egan departed shortly afterwards, taking the last echoes of Sir William's sagacity with him.

There was no doubting Ford's financial commitment. Money poured in to fund new facilities and processes. Design-wise, though, the cars were mired in a timewarp based on a middle-aged American's view of what Jaguars should be – a stasis Sir William never tolerated even in his own middle age. In chasing the high volumes that rivals BMW and Mercedes-Benz were achieving, new cars like the S-type and X-type drew increasingly on Ford platforms. Once again, as Sir William espouses in his views on the specialist car's future in

TOP Jaguar's return to motor-sport was with the revitalised XJ-S in the European Touring Car Championship, where it proved an immediate winner.

ABOVE The Jaguar XJR-9 won the 1988 24 Hours of Le Mans, and the World Sportscar Championship with it.

BELOW Designer Ian Callum, here with his new XK in 2006, had been an admirer of Lyons since childhood.

BOTTOM Controversial but a fine sports saloon nonetheless, the new S-Type arrived in 1998.

his 1969 address, 'a liking for a car which is different' had to be skilfully handled in an era of increasing standardisation. Nonetheless, the Jaguars on offer at the turn of the century were pretty much world-class in their capabilities and integrity. There was much to be thankful for… but then yet another shock to the Jaguar system was coming.

In 2008 a strategic upheaval at Ford saw Jaguar sold to Indian conglomerate Tata. It was immediately brought together in Tata's new Jaguar Land Rover (JLR) subsidiary. The company became Indian-owned, but was now given the freedom to forge its own distinctive path. With its three large manufacturing facilities at Castle Bromwich, Solihull and Halewood, its two design centres at Gaydon, Warwickshire and Whitley, Coventry, and two of the greatest marque names in the whole of motoring history, JLR promised an exciting future.

Jaguar did indeed enter a new golden era. Ian Callum had joined as design head from Aston Martin, a gifted shaper of cars who was himself in awe of Sir William's own innate skills, and built back Jaguar's individuality with a string of acclaimed saloons and sports cars. There were things that the market wanted and couldn't reasonably be refused, such as diesel engines and estate cars. There were inevitable changes that Sir William would have been sanguine about, like the closure of the crumbling Browns Lane plant, and the quiet axing of the Daimler sister marque.

The founder's distant mantra of driving forward new technology was tackled too. In 2013 JLR was revealed as the most significant investor in research and development in the British motor industry, with £3bn lavished on an avalanche of new products.

One of these was the 2015 F-Pace, Jaguar's first ever sport-utility vehicle (SUV) and coming 18 years after BMW's X5. Many marque aficionados deplored it but within a year it was the best-selling Jaguar of all, and was soon joined by a smaller running mate, the E-Pace. A clever design system using modular aluminium structures meant that many unseen components were shared with the more traditional Jaguar XE and XF cars, but also various Land Rover and Range Rover models which sold in much, much higher volumes than the Jags. Then in 2018 came the ell-electric Jaguar I-Pace, a car just as adventurous in its own way as the D-type, E-type and XJ220; Britain's luxurious alternative to a Tesla.

These vehicles should have swelled Jaguar. Instead, and strangely, they've hamstrung it. Buyers deserted the traditional saloons for the SUVs, but even more have tended to choose a Range Rover instead. The I-Pace, meantime, while brave, was expensive to develop and failed to meet sales expectations. Throw in the global pandemic and the uncertainty about the electric car's future and the wind has deserted Jaguar's sails once again. All the current cars are shortly to be dropped, and the plan is to take Jaguar a long way up-market as an electric ultra-luxury car in the Bentley echelon. This really is a shift in mindset that Sir William might have been aghast at. His SS 2½-litre saloon – the one he mentions in his address being unveiled to gasps at the Mayfair Hotel in 1935 – was

TOP Jaguar XF, introduced in 2007, proved a worldwide hit.

ABOVE New Jaguar XJ, launched in 2010 and with an entirely aluminium structure.

OPPOSITE Jaguar F-Pace SUV, at one stage the marque's best-selling car.

supposed to be a Bentley-style car for a third of the price…

So the pressing question: 'What is a Jaguar meant to be?' has now arisen, and the company has stoked the debate by revealing a concept coupé with striking proportions inside and out, and an electric motor. It was named Type 00. The furore around it, just a concept car like countless others in motoring history, created a media storm at the end of 2024, the like of which has rarely been seen before. Politicians and celebrities waded in; TV stations, websites and newspapers used it to fill airtime and space; and social media erupted in a custard-pie fight of opinion, goading and rancour. Jaguar really matters to people. That is clear.

The four-door GT, with a reported 986bhp of all-electric power – equivalent to four times that of a high-tune edition of Lyons's beloved XK straight-six, the petrol-burning crucible of Jaguar's post-war success – was scheduled to go on sale by the end of 2026, at a price of £100,000-plus. The man now in charge of the Jaguar brand, managing director Rawdon Glover, in a March 2025 interview with *Autocar* magazine, described its development as "the complete opposite of how everything used to work." He also anticipated an "elegant sunset" as the outgoing range was wound-down. "There's no real playbook for that, because nobody else has done it before. We will have this period now of 'breathing space' to really build the [new] brand, the awareness, the interest, before we actually start taking orders further down the track."

All of that would possibly have been perplexing to Sir William, whose world-famous business was a steady – if always imaginative – evolution. And yet, although physical links were set to be broken, Mr Glover's respect for Jaguar's character and historical importance was obvious. He claimed teams of chassis engineers had spent many days driving classic models to soak up what made them special and "absolutely inherently Jaguar," and that "…For many, the reason they're here is because their grandfather worked at Jaguar, their father worked here, and they have an affinity with it and they are deeply passionate about what we do.

"We've looked at our history and what we're going to be doing is not a literal interpretation. If you're looking for a literal interpretation, we'd have just gone and done an E-type 'resto-mod' and been rightly criticised. If you look at those moments in Jaguar's history when it was really successful and really relevant, culturally, socially, commercially, it's because it was very, very clear about what it was about. We should take Jaguar back to a positioning of when it was much more successful in the marketplace and really try and restore that real lustre that the brand definitely had, and we definitely see. But the interesting thing about Jaguar is most of the affinity tends to be with what we've done historically, not what we've been doing recently."

As this book goes to press, then, the future shape of Jaguar is hugely anticipated.

OV16 NPJ

JBS 768

OPPOSITE Jaguar's I-Pace of 2018, an all-electric challenge to Tesla.

OVERLEAF Future in the pink? Jaguar Concept 00 seeks to rewrite the marque's rulebook; Sir William Lyons himself always understood the need to move on…

And so it is timely and apposite that Sir William Lyons' own reflections on building his car business are reproduced here, for the first time in full and 'from the horse's mouth'. If you want to understand how Mr Jaguar himself saw things, then here it is.

There are many published marque histories on Jaguar, both lightweight and extraordinarily detailed. There are books on specific models, even single cars, and also on the marque's fabulous exploits and achievements on the race track. Sir William's address to the Institute, to be sure, is not a comprehensive history. If anything, it is an easy-to-digest insight into his business and how he saw the way ahead, culminating at the point where the Jaguar XJ6 represents everything he achieved.

Some famous models, such as the XK 140, XK 150 and XKSS, don't merit even his passing mention, and nor does the astonishing Mark X super-saloon of 1961, whose design and impact is often overlooked anyway. The E-type, or 'E' Type as he more quaintly puts it, gets a mention for 95% of its sales going to the USA, and not its performance or even its genesis arising from the D-type. He was far too self-effacing to mention his 1956 knighthood for Jaguar's spectacular success in exports.

The speaker devotes a surprising amount of detail to his move, following the purchase of Daimler and Guy, into commercial vehicles. It's interesting to hear how evidently proud he was of the Fleetline bus and the Big J lorries, and how he made the most of everything that came with his astute company purchases in the mid 1960s. As well as Jaguars there was a large industrial complex here, making all kinds of unexpected things – or, at least, that's what you discover if you've only associated this man with cars.

Sir William does name-check many key people in Jaguar's history, with the one rather extraordinary omission of the name of his founding partner, William Walmsley, who for whatever shortcomings he may have had in business was willing – like Andrew Ridgley to George Michael in Wham! – to stand aside so the more singular talent could take wing and soar.

Another thing he fails to do, because of course it was no-one's business in relation to the history of Jaguar, was give any details of his own early years. It's illuminating to know them: born in Blackpool on 4 September 1901, his father William Lyons was an Irish immigrant who ran a musical instrument shop, and his mother Minnie was from a mill-owning family. They were modestly well off, at best, and their son went to the nearby secondary Arnold School, where he was apparently a diligent student. Through his father's connections, he gained an engineering apprenticeship at Manchester's Crossley Motors, and a city technical school, but left at 19 to work as a car salesman for a Blackpool garage.

He bought and tinkered with an old Sunbeam motorbike, and shared his love of 'bikes with near-neighbour William Walmsley, who reconditioned ex-military WWI models to sell on. Walmsley also made his own, remarkably stylish sidecars, and William Lyons bought one for his latest steed, a Norton. That gave the two friends the idea to become partners; Lyons was 21, Walmsley ten years his senior. The rest, as the cliché has it, really is history.

Sir William Lyons' rare personal account of his life and ambitions, delivered to the enraptured Institute of the Motor Industry audience when the Beatles were still jamming together and pounds, shillings and pence hadn't yet been decimalised, is the authentic one. Ian Cooling, a leading seller of Jaguar memorabilia and collectables, occasionally has a rare copy of this text, with its original folder, in one of his on-line auctions. He wrote: "This is one of the seminal papers on the Company history. I was told by Andrew Whyte [former Jaguar PR executive and author] that, apart from some fact-checking and general tidying-up that he carried out, this paper is essentially Sir William's own words. As such, it is unique.' And, of course, so it remains.

INDEX